Visiting the Past

Hadrian's Wall

Jane Shuter

www.heinemann.co.uk
Visit our website to find out more information about **Heinemann Library** books.

To order:
☎ Phone 44 (0) 1865 888066
 Send a fax to 44 (0) 1865 314091
💻 Visit the Heinemann Bookshop at www.heinemann.co.uk to browse our catalogue and order online.

First published in Great Britain by Heinemann Library,

Halley Court, Jordan Hill, Oxford OX2 8EJ,

a division of Reed Educational and Professional Publishing Ltd.

Heinemann is a registered trademark of Reed Educational & Professional Publishing Limited.

OXFORD MELBOURNE AUCKLAND JOHANNESBURG BLANTYRE GABORONE
IBADAN PORTSMOUTH NH (USA) CHICAGO

© Reed Educational and Professional Publishing Ltd 1999
The moral right of the proprietor has been asserted.

Designed by Visual Image
Illustrations by Visual Image
Printed in Hong Kong

ISBN 0 431 02773 0 (hardback)   ISBN 0 431 02780 3 (paperback)
03 02 01 00 99   04 03 02 01 00
10 9 8 7 6 5 4 3 2 1   10 9 8 7 6 5 4 3 2 1

British Library Cataloguing in Publication Data

Shuter, Jane
    Hadrian's Wall. – (Visiting the past)
    1. Romans – England – Juvenile literature 2. Hadrian's Wall (England)
    – Juvenile literature
    I. Title
    936.2'881

Acknowledgements

The Publishers would like to thank Terry Griffiths and Magnet Harlequin by arrangement with English Heritage, the National Trust and the Vindolanda Trust for permission to reproduce all photographs, with the exception of pages 14, 18 and 20, reproduced with permission of Terry Griffiths and Magnet Harlequin by arrangement with Corbridge Museum. The photographs on pages 24, 25 (middle) and 27 (lower) are reproduced with permission of Vindolanda Museum.

Cover photograph reproduced with permission of Terry Griffiths and Magnet Harlequin

The Publishers would like to thank Joe Scott for his comments in the preparation of this title.

Every effort has been made to contact copyright holders of any material reproduced in this book. Any omissions will be rectified in subsequent printings if notice is given to the Publisher.

Any words appearing in the text in bold, **like this**, are explained in the Glossary.

Contents

The edges of empire

Hadrian's Wall stretches 117 kilometres from one side of Britain to the other, from the River Tyne in the east to the Solway Firth in the west. In some places its path is barely visible through the grass; in others it remains thick, solid and imposing. Every year hundreds of people walk along parts of the Wall, some even try to follow it from one side of the country to the other.

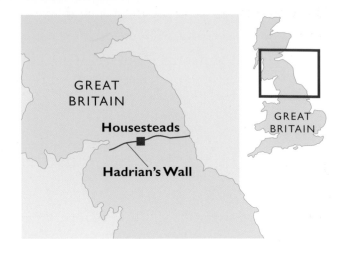

Others travel by car to visit the remains of forts and settlements scattered along the Wall. Who built Hadrian's Wall, and why?

Hadrian's Wall was begun in AD122; built on the orders of the Roman Emperor Hadrian. The **Roman Empire** had reached out from Italy to cover a vast area, circling the Mediterranean Sea and stretching from Britain in the north to Egypt in the south. It seemed as if the Roman Empire would never stop growing; but it did and then the places most vulnerable to attacks by other groups were the edges of the Empire, such as the north of Britain.

There had been various defensive **fortifications** in northern Britain before, to keep the 'barbarians' (non–Romans) at bay. On a visit to Britain in about AD121, Hadrian announced that there had to be a permanent line of defence – a wall from sea to sea, with sixteen forts, many smaller fortifications and permanent **garrisons** of soldiers, to 'separate the Romans from the barbarians'.

Hadrian's Wall, looking west from Housesteads Fort. The Wall followed the line of the hills, using the steep slope as a natural defence. It also had a defensive ditch on either side.

Defending the Empire

The Wall was not built all at once, and was not the same all along its length. There was also more to the defences than just the Wall. The main road, the Stanegate, that ran to the south of Hadrian's Wall, had several large military towns on it, which acted as back-up to the Wall. There were also two deep ditches on either side of the Wall, making it difficult to cross at anywhere other than the guarded crossing-points. In this way, the Romans were able to keep a close eye on the activities of local people.

Reconstructions at Vindolanda, a Roman fort and **civilian** settlement on the other side of the Stanegate from Hadrian's Wall, show what the Wall would have looked like. The Wall was 6.4 metres high and probably had a walkway on the southern side that was 4.8 metres high. Little evidence of this walkway survives, so some historians think there may not have been one.

The Wall from Birdoswald to Bowness was originally made of stacked turf with wooden fortifications. These were later rebuilt in stone.

You can see how the natural-looking bank was made up of stacked turf.

A stone turret and part of the Wall, 2.4 m thick. When the Wall was begun it was supposed to be 3 m thick and a 3 m thick foundation was laid to show the course the Wall was to take. But the need for speed and the problem of getting supplies of stone meant that most of the Wall was built 2.4 m thick – it was even as little as 1.8 m thick in places.

Who built the Wall?

Hadrian's Wall was built by soldiers, not workmen. Each legion (see below) built a section about eight kilometres long. When their sections were completed they added a stone which said who had built it. Building work was as tightly controlled as any other part of life in the highly organized Roman army.

This stone tells us that the century [shown by a backwards C] Florinus built a section of the Wall 22 paces long.

The whole Wall used over 1,000,000 cubic metres of stone, every piece of which had to be **quarried**, shaped and transported to the right place, where the foundations were already in place. All this work, including levelling the ground enough to build solid foundations, only took about six years, although there were constant repairs and rebuildings after that. This is an amazing feat considering that the Romans had no mechanical diggers or cranes, no heavy lifting machinery and no trucks to transport the stone needed for the Wall.

The Roman army

The Roman army was organized in *legions*.

Each *legion* was made up of ten *cohorts* of soldiers and several hundred **civilians**: **clerks** who kept the records, master builders, surveyors, engineers, carpenters and other specialists that made the army **self-sufficient**.

Each *cohort* was made up of ten **centuries**.

Each *century* was made up of about 80 men, under an officer called the **centurion**. These men were organized into groups of eight, called a *tent* [that was how many each army tent held].

Each *century* had its own **standard** – a long pole with a decorative design on the top. Each *legion* also had an imperial standard, topped with an eagle design, to remind them of their loyalty to Rome.

Manning the Wall

Roman **legionaries** built the Wall, but it was manned by **auxiliaries** – troops raised in lands conquered by Rome. In the case of Hadrian's Wall, the troops were mostly from northern Europe and Britain itself. Some senior officers and administrators came from Italy.

So did the Wall work? Yes, it seemed to. It made the point that this was the edge of the Empire. It was solid and well-manned – by about 14,000 soldiers at full strength. This was enough to impress the tribes to the north and south and to deter attacks. The attacks that were made on the Wall were often made when soldiers had left the Wall to deal with trouble in other parts of the Empire. Hadrian's Wall also provided the Roman army with a base from which to patrol further north, and keep watch on the 'barbarian' tribes there. The Romans even made peace **treaties** with some tribes, possibly helped by the strength of the Wall.

The **masons** in charge of the building work would mark on the foundation stones where the wall line would run. Here you can see the marks for the west gate at Housesteads Fort.

These building tools were found on the Wall. They are, from left to right: a nail, a plumb bob (hung from a piece of string to check things are straight), a chisel, a trowel and a slater's hammer.

Some roofs were tiled with stone slates. The roofs of more important buildings, the hospital and headquarters at Housesteads Fort for example, were roofed with **terracotta** tiles like these.

Changes on the Wall

The Emperor who ruled after Hadrian, called Antoninus Pius, had another wall built further north, the Antonine Wall, in about AD141. It was shorter (58 kilometres) but in more dangerous territory than Hadrian's Wall, so it needed more forts and more men. The Antonine Wall was abandoned after only fourteen years. Hadrian's Wall was once again the front line.

Daily life on the Wall also changed in this period. As soldiers moved about less, **civilian** settlements grew. Some of the soldiers married among the local people and had families. All this lessened the sense that the Wall was in danger. It was then, in AD367, that one of the most serious attacks on the Wall occurred. It was suppressed, but the **Roman Empire** was shrinking, and faraway Britain was one of the first places to be abandoned.

By AD410 no more money was sent from Rome to pay the soldiers, and no more taxes were collected in Britain. After 300 years of being a base for keeping the local people in order, the Wall was slowly but surely absorbed into local life.

So what does the Wall today tell us about what it was like to be a soldier on Hadrian's Wall? The evidence for life on duty in a fort mostly comes from Housesteads Fort. The evidence about life off duty, in the civilian settlements that grew up around the forts, mostly comes from the settlement at Vindolanda.

Archaeologists are excavating parts of the Wall all the time. Each excavation helps our understanding of life on the Wall. The picture on the right shows what Housesteads Fort might have looked like.

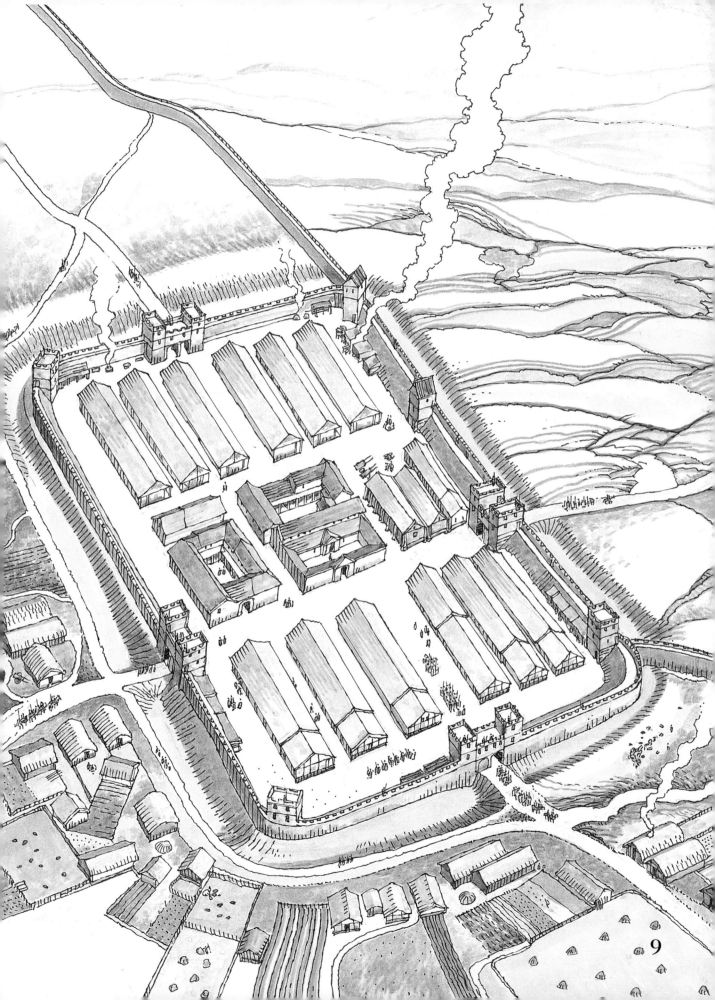

A home from home

Ordinary soldiers lived in the **barracks**, which were at the east and west ends of the fort. The barracks were not built entirely of stone, like the hospital, headquarters and **granary**. They were built on a stone base, much of which is still there. **Archaeologists** have found evidence that the walls of the barracks were mainly wood and plaster, with slate roofs and probably wooden floors. Not all of the barrack blocks were used as living quarters. One of them was certainly used as a workshop at some time and another went through several changes, being used at different times as store, armoury and stables, as well as barracks.

The earliest barracks were long buildings divided into ten units, each housing up to eight soldiers. They were divided into a sleeping area, at the back, and a storage area, at the front. At one end of the barrack there was a separate, wider set of rooms for the **centurion** in charge, with enough room to house his slaves, sometimes even his family. Shortly before AD300 the barracks were rebuilt as smaller units with lanes between them.

A single barrack block

The little cross lanes show how a single barrack was split up into smaller units.

The Commandant's house

Centurions had more living space than ordinary soldiers, but the Commandant of the fort lived in a different style altogether. His house, the largest single building in the fort, was on the southern side of the central block of official buildings. It was built around a central open courtyard and had enough room for the Commandant, his family and his slaves. It even had stables for his horses. Excavations show that half the house (the family rooms) was built from stone and the rest from wood and plaster, although the wood and plaster part was later rebuilt in stone.

stables

open courtyard

toilets

The Commandant had his own kitchen. A raised oven was built on to the stone platform.

The family dining-room was heated by a **hypocaust** system.

13

Feeding an army

Grain was one of the most important foods for the army. It was made into both porridge and bread, a big part of the soldiers' daily diet. There were big **quern-stones** for grinding the grain into flour. Many soldiers were also issued with portable grindstones to grind their own grain ration. Bakehouses and ovens were situated against the walls near the **barracks** – not in the barracks because of the risk of fire.

Lists of army stores that have survived from the time tell us about the food provided for the soldiers. As well as bread and porridge, they ate cheese, vegetables and fruit each day. They only ate meat occasionally. They drank mainly wine, which was brought from Roman-occupied France and Spain.

A quern-stone for grinding grain, from Corbridge Museum. A **convex** stone of a similar size would have been placed under this one. Grain was poured into a central hole and a handle was turned, moving the top stone. The pressure crushed the grain into flour, which came out at the side. The grooves are thought to have been made to let the flour out.

The **granaries** were used mainly for storing grain, although it is likely that all the food for the fort was stored here.

The ground level of the granary was raised on stone pillars; to keep out the damp. This also helped to keep rats and mice out.

Under-floor **ventilation** was provided by these vents.

The big doors were heavy wood. The door stop on the right kept mice out. The holes were for bolts, which kept people out.

Archaeologists think there probably was a second storey, because the side walls are thick and have extra supporting **buttresses**, which would not have been needed on a single-storey building.

15

Keeping clean and healthy

It was important for soldiers to be fit. They were fed a healthy diet. Training **drills**, long marches and building work on the Wall gave them plenty of exercise. **Hygiene** was also very important. Soldiers were expected to wash themselves, and their clothes, regularly. Toilet blocks were also provided, with running water and drains for the **sewage**.

It was important to have a good supply of clean water. Rain-water was carefully collected and saved. Water that ran off the roofs of the **barracks** was collected in **gullies** that ran off to stone tanks. Any dirt settled at the bottom of the tanks.

At Housesteads Fort, up on a rocky ridge, the Romans could not dig wells. The rock was too hard to dig through. They had to rely on collecting rain-water in stone tanks scattered around the site. They took water from a nearby stream too.

At Vindolanda, which is quite low-lying, the Romans dug wells for fresh water. They also collected rain-water in tanks.

Roman toilets

The toilet block at Housesteads is very well preserved, and shows how they worked. The men sat on a bench that ran along three sides of the block. One of the stone **corbels** that supported the seats is still in place (**A**) and stones have been laid (**B**) to show the level of the floor.

Water to clean away the sewage came from a stone tank and ran under the floor. The ground level sloped from the highest point where the water came in (**C**) to the point where the sewage drained out through a hole in the wall (**D**).

The Romans did not use toilet paper. In Italy, they used pieces of sponge wrapped around a stick, some of which have survived. It would have been expensive to import sponges to Britain for this. **Archaeologists** think they used local moss instead. They rinsed this out in a shallow gully that ran around the block (**E**). Fresh water for the gully came from a stone tank, through a channel (**F**) into the block. Stone troughs of water were provided for hand washing (**G**).

A complex system of drains carried rain-water to the toilets.

Treating the sick

Although the army went to a lot of trouble to make sure their soldiers stayed fit, most people were sick from time to time. They caught diseases. They got boils, sore teeth, minor burns and wounds. Soldiers could also be more severely wounded in battle. So there were medical teams for each unit of the Roman army, each with their own trained officer, and the main forts often had a hospital.

Roman doctors used herbal medicines and ointments; they even knew of herbal **anaesthetics** (belladonna) and **antiseptics** (turpentine). They had a whole range of surgical equipment from probes and scalpels, for dealing with boils, to heavy saws, for amputating limbs. However, they turned to surgery only as a last resort. They knew that, especially in cases of major surgery, the shock of the operation, or infections that set in after, meant the patient was just as likely to die after surgery.

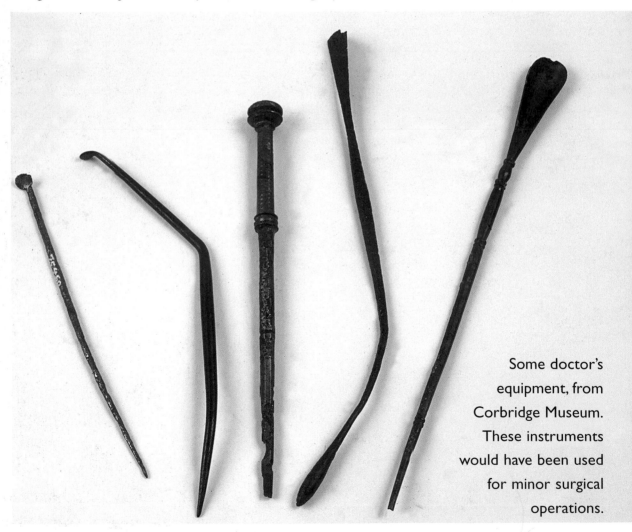

Some doctor's equipment, from Corbridge Museum. These instruments would have been used for minor surgical operations.

The hospital at Housesteads

paved central courtyard, open to the sky

This may have been the operating theatre.

The smaller rooms (below) were wards where the patients were treated.

The hospital had its own toilets and drainage system.

Off duty

Much of a Roman soldier's life on Hadrian's Wall revolved around the fort he was stationed at and his military duties. But even Roman soldiers got some time off, and there was life outside the fort. The soldiers went outside the fort to do their military exercises and training. The **bathhouse** was usually sited outside the fort too, because it took up a lot of space. Soldiers were expected to use the bathhouse regularly.

Many Roman forts developed a **civilian** settlement around their walls, providing services for the soldiers ranging from drinking houses to shoe shops. There might also be a temple. Indeed, some civilian settlements grew to be as big as the fort itself. Others were more basic, just a bathhouse and a few houses.

A glass oil jar found at Corbridge. The Romans did not use soap to wash with. Instead, they oiled their bodies and then scraped off the oil (and any dirt) with a metal scraper called a strigil.

The military bathhouse at Vindolanda.

Bathers left their clothes in the changing room (**A**). They then took some exercise (**B**) and moved on into the warm room (**C**), where they sat to warm up. They moved on to the hot, steamy room (**D**), where they got very sweaty, then oiled and scraped themselves in the hot, dry room (**E**) before a warm bath (**F**). Finally, they had a quick plunge into the cold pool (**G**), to close up their **pores** before dressing.

The cold bath. You can see where the water feeds in on the far side.

Houses and homes

The **civilians'** houses at Vindolanda varied in size according to the wealth and importance of the inhabitants. Many of the buildings at Vindolanda changed use over time; there was a lot of rebuilding. As well as new building, houses were also altered to hold more or fewer families. Some houses were also workshops and shops.

A long **barrack** house at Vindolanda, possibly quarters for married soldiers, whose wives and families would not have been allowed to live in the barracks inside the fort.

A house where each room belonged to a different family (left). You can still see the remains of stone fireplaces in each room.

This house (right) is thought to have once been half of a large house, split in two by a corridor. The house was later divided into two houses.

The building now thought to be the Commandant's house is so large that it was at first thought to be an inn. Vindolanda was not on the Wall itself, but on the Stanegate, the main road that ran along the Wall. This would have made it a natural stopping place for people travelling along the Wall. It is still possible that the house began its life as an inn, but **archaeologists** think it was probably used as a home by Commandants in the later years of the Roman occupation of Britain.

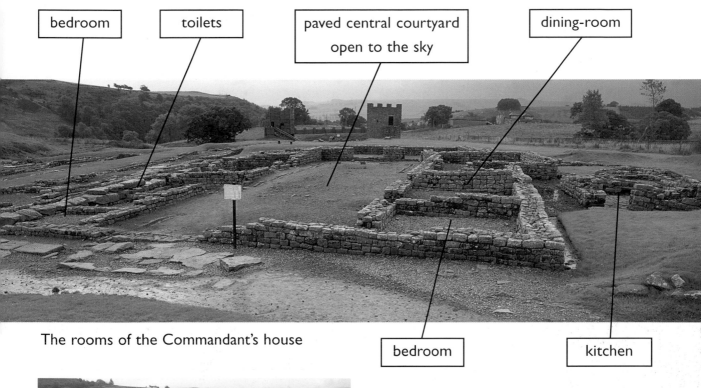

bedroom

toilets

paved central courtyard open to the sky

dining-room

bedroom

kitchen

The rooms of the Commandant's house

The bath complex took up the whole of one end of the house.

Although there were kitchens in the house itself, the ovens were built outside, to reduce the fire risk.

Shopping in Vindolanda

Vindolanda had various shops, selling such things as shoes and pottery. Some of these things were made in workshops on the site – there are remains to show that bronze-making and leather-working went on here. Much of the food on sale was grown locally: fruit and vegetables, cheese and milk, meat and honey. Only the Commandant's family would have been able to afford goods brought in from other countries or cities, where there were craftsmen producing finer goods.

It is likely that Vindolanda had its own potters, making simple bowls and jugs for everyday use. Pottery has been found there that could have been locally made. There are tools that suggest there were local woodworkers and builders too. The **civilians** would also have run their own eating and drinking houses, sold their own vegetables and livestock and some may have made enough fabric to have extra to sell.

This piece of a glass found at Vindolanda, painted with **gladiators**, was made in Cologne, Germany. It would have been very expensive and must have belonged to the Commandant of the fort.

Although there is no surviving evidence at Vindolanda, the shops probably had shutters that ran along a shutter groove and opened at the side of the house. This shutter groove and bolt hole are from a shop at Housesteads, which had a smaller civilian settlement just outside the walls.

These scraps of bronze were found on the site of a bronzeworks at Vindolanda.

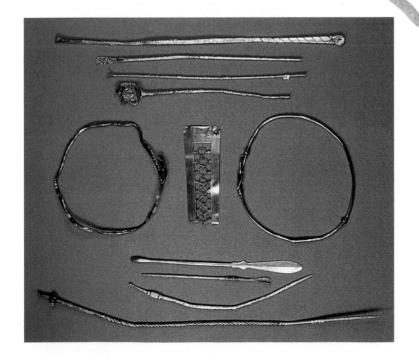

The shops at Vindolanda would only have sold very basic goods. To buy something as well made as this inkwell, people would have had to travel to the nearest big town.

Praying and playing

Civilian settlements usually had at least one temple, with altars to various gods. Some places also had a temple or shrine to Mithras, the Persian sun god who was very popular with Roman soldiers and who was worshipped in secret ceremonies. Other Roman gods and goddesses were worshipped widely and openly by anyone who chose to do so.

Burying the dead

Roman law said that cemeteries must be built outside the fort, away from the civilian settlements. They were often sited near roads, for easy access. People who were wealthy enough set up memorial stones to the dead along the main roads leading into forts or settlements.

An altar to Mars, the god of war, which was found at Housesteads.

Soldiers did have some spare time to amuse themselves, when they were not on duty, bathing, shopping or worshipping. Some civilians brewed beer and sold it from their homes, so soldiers could, and did, go drinking, although drunkenness was frowned on by the army.

Soldiers also liked to play various dice and board games. Examples of these have been found in several sites along Hadrian's Wall. While soldiers were not supposed to gamble their pay away on games like this, they often did. Some dice have been found that are 'loaded', or unevenly weighted so that they are more likely to fall on some numbers than others. Some gamblers obviously believed in improving their chances!

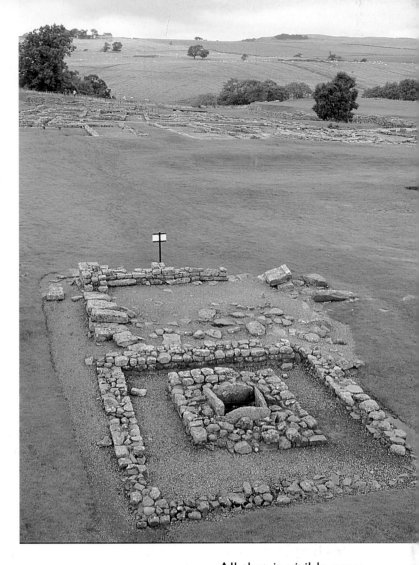

All that is visible now of the cemetery at Vindolanda are the remains of two imposing tombs.

A gameboard, pieces and dice found at Vindolanda. The dice are loaded, so that the numbers 6 and 1 come up most often!

Timeline

AD43	Romans conquer Britain and begin to settle there
122	Hadrian's Wall begun
141	Antonine Wall begun
155	Antonine Wall abandoned
251	Goths invade Gaul (modern France). The **Roman Empire** is no longer easy to control.
285	Emperor Diocletian splits the Empire into two parts, to be ruled by two different emperors
296	Many troops taken from Hadrian's Wall to keep peace closer to Rome. The Wall is attacked by northern tribes.
367	Fiercest attacks on Hadrian's Wall, by peoples from the north and from outside Britain. The Wall is seriously damaged for the first time.
410	Romans stop sending money to Britain to pay troops. No more money is collected from the local people. Hadrian's Wall is slowly absorbed into local life.

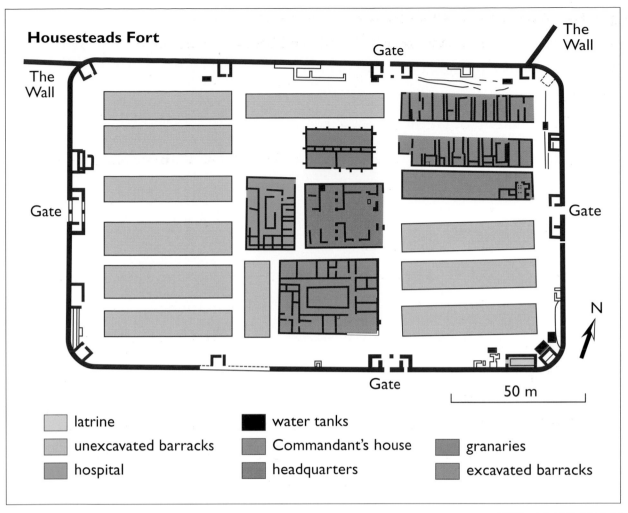

Housesteads Fort

The Wall

Gate

The Wall

The Wall

Gate

Gate

Gate

N

Gate

50 m

	latrine		water tanks		granaries
	unexcavated barracks		Commandant's house		excavated barracks
	hospital		headquarters		

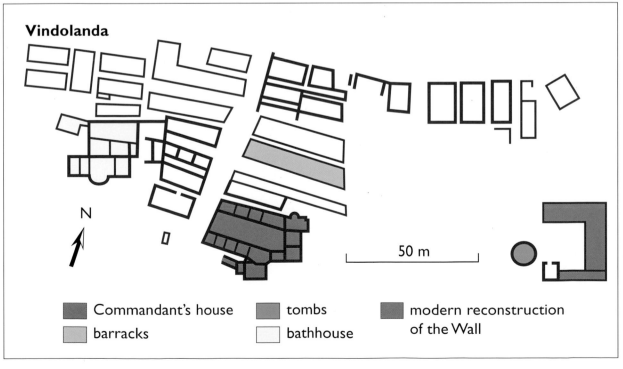

Vindolanda

N

50 m

	Commandant's house		tombs		modern reconstruction of the Wall
	barracks		bathhouse		

Glossary

anaesthetic substance that stops a person feeling pain

antiseptic substance that kill germs and bacteria and stops infection spreading

archaeologist person who studies the past by looking at ancient ruins and remains

auxiliary Roman soldier who was not a Roman citizen, often recruited from the lands the Romans conquered

barracks building where soldiers live as a group

bathhouse in Roman times, a place where people washed and exercised together

buttress structure built against a wall to strengthen it

centurion an officer in the Roman army, in charge of a century (80 men)

century unit of the Roman army

civilian person who is not in the armed forces. Civilian settlements along the wall were places where ordinary people lived.

clerk an official record-keeper

convex curved outwards like the outer surface of a ball

corbel piece of stone or wood jutting out from a wall in order to support a weight

drill method of training soldiers

fortification structure that makes a place more secure from attack. These can be walls, castles or forts.

garrison troops put into a fort or town to guard the surrounding area

gladiator trained performer who fights with a sword or other weapon as a form of entertainment

granary a place where grain is stored

gully man-made channel to drain water

hygiene keeping clean

hypocaust a system of heating where the floor of a room is supported on pillars and the air in the space under the floor is heated. The hot air rises and warms the room above.

infantry soldiers who fight on foot with light weapons

legionary Roman soldier who was also a Roman citizen

mason someone who carves stone

pore tiny opening in the skin which can be blocked by dirt. Heat opens the pores up, so the dirt can be washed off, but leaves them open so more dirt can get in. Cold closes the pores up.

quarry place where stone is dug from the ground

quern-stone large stone used for grinding corn

Roman Empire the area conquered by the Roman armies, beginning in about 510BC, which circled the Mediterranean Sea and stretched from Britain in the north to Egypt in the south. Britain was one of the edges of the Empire, one of the last places to be conquered and one of the first places to be left. The Romans invaded Britain in AD43 and left in AD410.

self-sufficient not relying on anyone else to live, for example by growing your own food

sewage waste matter carried away in drains and sewers

standard a long pole which carried an emblem for each century of the Roman army. It was important for ceremonies, but also in battle so soldiers could tell where their comrades were by the position of the standard.

terracotta a type of reddish-brown pottery

treaty any agreement made between groups of people or countries

ventilation allowing air to move freely around a room or space

*I*ndex